Snoopy's Secret Code Book

by

Charles M. Schulz
Kathryn Wentzel Lumley

Holt, Rinehart and Winston, Inc.
New York Toronto London Sydney

Pig Pen

SBN: 03-086069-5
12345 071 987654321

Hello Reader,

Welcome to Snoopy's book.
Turn the page. Take a look.

Meet Snoopy's friends. Learn their names.
Read cartoons and make up games.

Snoopy's Secret Code Book's clues
Are the colors that we use.

When looking for vowels, be sure to stop
At pages with the gold on top.

When consonants are what you need
Look for the green before you read.

Cartoons have red clues; words do, too.
Red is Snoopy's favorite clue.

Directions tell you what to do
To make the red clues work for you.

Use these clues without delay,
Learn new words to spell and say.

Peppermint Patty

Linus

Violet

Schroeder

José Peterson

Thibault

Lucy

2

Woodstock

Franklin Sally Brown Charlie Brown

Snoopy

SCHULZ

Page Clues for Spelling

Some spellings for the sounds we give to f :

f

Some spellings for the sounds we give to g :

g

Some spellings for the sounds we give to h :

h

Some spellings for the sounds we give to i :

i

Some spellings for the sounds we give to j :

j

Some spellings for the sounds we give to k :

k

Some spellings for the sounds we give to v :

v v 88

Some spellings for the sounds we give to w :

w

w 90   ow 93
wr 92   ew 93
wh 92   aw 93

Some spellings for the sounds we give to x :

x x 94

Some spellings for the sounds we give to y :

y y 98

Some spellings for the sounds we give to z :

z

z 102   x 96
s 79

Aa *Aa*

caps

cake

This word can be fun to say. Say it giving the a the same sound you give to the a in cap.

Augh!

Now say the word giving the a the same sound you give to the a in cake.

Aaaughh!

Which way do you like better?

10

Say these words. Give the a
in these words the same
sound that you give the a
in cap.

flag	and
crabby	grab
bat	candle

Say these words.
Give the a in these words
the same sound that you give
to the a in cake.

hate	plane
face	date
cave	bake

Aa *Aa*

vowel

Give the **a** in these words the same sound you give to the **a** in c**a**ke. Notice the different spellings.

ay

pl**ay**

s**ay**
d**ay**
st**ay**

ai

r**ai**n

br**ai**n
pl**ai**n
tr**ai**n

aigh

str**aigh**t

12

bat

tu**b**

ba**b**y

Say these words.

beagle   grab

baseball   book

garbage   bark

THE BLANKET I CAN SEE....BUT THE THUMB, NO!

THAT CONSTANT SLURPING SIMPLY NAUSEATES ME!

I DON'T THINK I'M GOING TO BE ABLE TO STAND IT....

THERE MUST BE HUNDREDS OF TRAVEL AGENTS WHO WOULD BE ONLY TOO GLAD TO GUIDE YOU TO THE OTHER SIDE OF THE WORLD!

bl

blah!

blue
black
blanket
blockhead

br

branch

broom
bright
break
bread

When you say these words do not give any sound to the **b**.

clim**b**

thum**b**
dum**b**
lim**b**

Say these words. Give **c** the same sound as you
give **k** in **k**iss.

castle

musi**c**

pi**c**nic

Say these words. When the c comes before e, i or y you often give it the same sound as you give the s in sit.

5 cents

Lucy

icicle

19

Cc *Cc*

Say these words, giving c the sound you give c in cap.

cat   cup

car   cookie

coconut   conservation

Say these words so that you give c the sound you give c in cent.

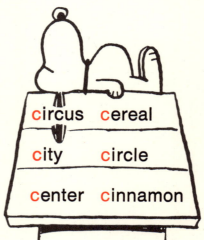

circus   cereal

city   circle

center   cinnamon

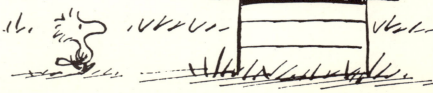

ch

Charlie Brown

chair
tea**ch**er
chicken
wat**ch**ing

When you say these words give the **ch** the same sound you give to **k** in **k**ite.

ch

stoma**ch**

tootha**ch**e

When you say some words which end with **ck**, give the **ck** the same sound as you give to **k** in **k**ite.

ck

ho**ck**ey

ba**ck**
ki**ck**

21

desk

bir**d**

can**d**y

Say these words.

dish feed

dirty read

dog Sunday

MY CARETAKER HAS A LITTLE TROUBLE WITH THE LAWN SPRINKLER...

23

dr

dress

drink
draw

When you say these **ld** words you give the **l** no sound.

ld

could

should
would

bed

she

Here's a favorite word of the Peanuts gang. Say it giving the e the same sound as the e in bed.

Bleah!

Say the word again but give the e the sound you give the e in she.

Which sounds best to you?

Bleah!

26

Ee **Ee**

Here are some words in which you give the e sound the same as the e in bed. Say them.

dr**e**ss	l**e**tter
n**e**st	t**e**nt
elf	inter**e**sting

EVERYONE IS SUPPOSED TO REPORT TO THE SKI HUT, CHARLIE BROWN

WE HAVE TO GET ALL OUR EQUIPMENT...

WHERE'S SNOOPY?

HE'S IN THE FITTING ROOM TRYING ON SKI BOOTS...

I MAY HAVE TO GO ONE SIZE SMALLER...

Ee *Ee*

Here are other spellings for the same sound as you give to the e in b**e**d.

ea  f**ea**thers

blockh**ea**d
l**ea**ther
br**ea**d

ie  fr**ie**nd

ay  s**ay**s

ai  s**ai**d

ag**ai**n

 28

In these words you give the e the same sound as you give the e in she.

e

he

be
we
me

These are other spellings for the same sound you give e in she.

ea

beagle

each
eat
dream

ee

teeth

bleep
sweet
bee

ie

piece

niece
believe

29

football

leaf

coffee

Say these words.

fish   if

fence   roof

face   jiffy

I'M HOOKED ON AUTUMN!

31

consonant

fr

Franklin

Frieda
freeze
friendly

fl

flower

flag
flew
fly

Sometimes the sound of **f** is shown by the letters **ph** as in **ph**one. See page 66.

Sometimes the sound of **f** is shown by the letters **gh** as in lau**gh**. See page 37.

32

g**uitar**

do**g**

SOMEDAY I SHOULD GO DOWN THERE...

g**ogg**les

germ

gingerbread

gypsy

Gg

consonant

Listen for the sound you give
to g as you say these words.
Make the g sound like the
g in guitar.

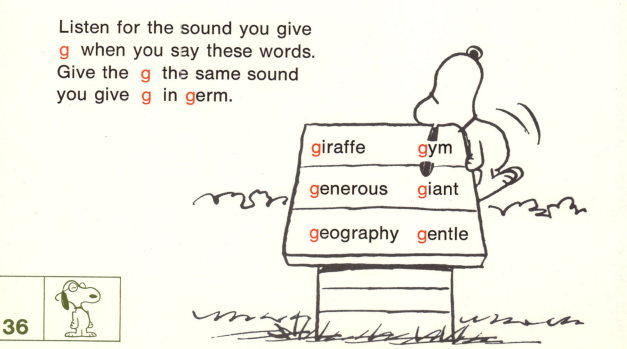

go	bigger
gone	giggle
wig	Pig Pen

Listen for the sound you give
g when you say these words.
Give the g the same sound
you give g in germ.

giraffe	gym
generous	giant
geography	gentle

 Gg

In these words give the **gh** the same sound as the
f in **f**ootball.

gh

lau**gh**

cou**gh**
rou**gh**
tou**gh**

gl

glove

glue
i**gl**oo

gr

grass

Great Pumpkin
green

Do you hear any **h** sound when you say these words?

house

Waa**h**!

Blaa**h**!

Say these words.

home	**h**eat
help	**h**imself
horse	**h**urt

NOW, THAT'S WHAT I CALL A BOOK REPORT..

THIS TIME I REALLY OUTDID MYSELF

I'VE GOT THE AUTHOR'S NAME, A BRIEF DESCRIPTION OF THE PLOT AND EVERYTHING...

I EVEN READ THE BOOK!

kiss

kite

Read this cartoon. Say h**i**c so that your **i** sounds like the sound you give **i** in k**i**ss.

h**i**c

h**i**c

Say h**i**c so that your **i** sounds like the sound you give **i** in k**i**te. Which sounds funnier to you?

Say these words. Give i the
same sound as your i in kiss.

sit   milk

fish   wing

hit   imagine

Say these words. Give i the
same sound as your i in kite.

five   bike

smile   I

idea   mind

Here are other spellings for the same sound that you give the i in kite.

ie  cried

tried
fried

igh  night

might
flight
bright

Sometimes y sounds like the i in kite. See page 100.

Jj *J j*

jelly

jumprope

44

Say these words

jeep	junk
jacket	jelly
jet	joyful

Often you will give words with **g** the same sound as you give the **j** in words. See page 35.

I THINK I'M WARPING!

Kk *Kk*

consonant

kite

book

jacket

46

Say these words.

ki**ck**	pee**k**
kid	**k**ey
bar**k**	**k**indergarten

Sometimes other letters stand for the sound you give
k . When you say these words, listen for the sound
you give **k** .

lk

LOOK OUT, EVERYBODY! I'M GONNA BE CRABBY FOR THE REST OF THE DAY!!

wa**lk**

ba**lk**
cha**lk**
ta**lk**

Give qu the sound you give k when you say this word.

qu  mos**qu**ito

Give kn the sound you give n when you say these words.

kn  **kn**ees

knight
knit
kneel
door**kn**ob

You often give c the same sound you give k as in **k**iss. See page 18.

letter

mea**l**

smi**l**e

Say these words.

SLAP!
SLAP!
WAP!!
SLAP!
SLAP!

Lucy	library
ladder	meal
lamp	ball

Give l no sound in these words.

palm	would
half	should
talk	calf

51

Mm *Mm*

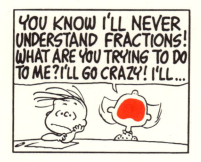

mouth

dru**m**

ca**m**era

Say these words.

milk summer

mail team

mud dime

THIS IS RIDICULOUS! IT'S ALMOST TEN-THIRTY!

WHERE IN THE WORLD IS HE?!

THIS IS OUTRAGEOUS!

NO ONE SHOULD HAVE TO WAIT UNTIL AFTER TEN O'CLOCK FOR HIS ENGLISH MUFFIN!

You hear only the sound of **m** when you say these words. Give the **b** no sound.

mb

thu**mb**

li**mb**
cli**mb**
nu**mb**

SORRY, NO DOGS ALLOWED IN THIS POOL!

SURELY YOU CAN'T MEAN **ME** ?!

nest

sun

dinner

Say these words.

nose   win

noise   sunny

window   fun

Now say this word. knew
Here you give kn the sound of n . See page 48.

Can you say this word? gnat
gn often is given the n sound.

Oo $\mathcal{O}o$

 box

 ghost

HE'S NOT VERY GOOD YET WITH A SCISSORS!

Here's a good word to practice the o sound. Say it first giving the o the sounds of the o in box.

Now say it making the o sound like the o in ghost. Which sounds best to you? Is there a better way to say it?

 Bonk!

 Bonk!

58

vowel

When you say these words give the **o** the same sound you give the **o** in b**o**x.

top	mop
doll	dot
clock	pocket

Here are some words in which you give the **o** the same sound as you give the **o** in gh**o**st.

go	potato
old	tomato
no	so

59

Give the **o** in these words the same sound you give the **o** in gh**o**st.

o

n**o**se

j**o**ke
h**o**le

oa

b**oa**t

g**oa**t
t**oa**st
gr**oa**n

ow

m**ow**er

gr**ow**
kn**ow**
sh**ow**

oe

t**oe**

Listen to the sound you give oo when you say these words.

oo

book

look
cook
foot

Oo *Oo*

Say these words.
Ou is given many different sounds when we say these words.

ou  through

ou  out

thousand
about

ou  house

ounce

62

Here are still more spellings with o's that you
give special sounds when you say them.

or

storm

sport
more
for

oor

floor

door

I DON'T THINK I'LL
TELL HER THAT..

our

four

court

YOU'LL PROBABLY MAKE A
FOOL OUT OF YOURSELF BY
USING THE WRONG FORK...

oo

moon

spoon
tooth
boot
cartoon

 Pow!

 cap

 Snoopy

Say these words.

pumpkin   supper

pizza   happy

ship   sleepy

HERE'S THE WORLD-FAMOUS HOCKEY GOALIE GUARDING THE NET..

AAUGH!

NOBODY SCORES!

pl

plant

plenty
play
please
plus

pr

SUDDENLY, I FEEL VERY FEMININE!

pretty

press
prize
prince
prop

Give **ph** the same sound as you give **f** in **f**at.

ph

AND STOP MAKING THOSE LONG-DISTANCE **PHONE** CALLS!

phone

photo
dolphin
geography

Qq *2 q*

question

q is seldom alone in a word. You most often find it before **u** .

Here are more words to say
and listen for the sound you
give to **qu** .

quick   **qu**een

quiet   s**qu**irrel

quarter   s**qu**eak

THIS IS MY INDIAN SUMMER DANCE..

ACTUALLY, I'M NEVER QUITE SURE JUST WHEN INDIAN SUMMER IS...SOME SAY IT'S THE WARM DAYS THAT FOLLOW THE FIRST FROST OF LATE AUTUMN..

I DON'T KNOW..MAYBE INDIAN SUMMER IS OVER.... MAYBE IT NEVER CAME...

ANYWAY, IT'S A NICE DAY, AND JUST IN CASE THIS IS INDIAN SUMMER, THIS IS MY INDIAN SUMMER DANCE!

Rr *Rr*

radio

ca**r**

ca**rr**ot

70

Here are more words to say.

rain   teacher

read   red

rink   parrot

A SPELLING BEE? THEY'RE GOING TO HAVE A CITY-WIDE SPELLING BEE?

I SHOULD ENTER IT...THAT'S THE SORT OF THING I NEED TO DO TO GAIN CONFIDENCE AND SELF-ESTEEM...

I THINK I'LL RAISE MY HAND AND VOLUNTEER...IT'LL BE GOOD FOR ME... I THINK I'LL JUST RAISE MY HAND AND VOLUNTEER...

MY HAND WON'T GO UP...IT'S SMARTER THAN I AM!

Rr *Rr*

Say these words and listen for the sounds you give
ir, er, or and ur. When r follows the vowels i, e, o and
u they sound the same.

er

her

mother
sister
brother

ir

dirty

sir
shirt
flirt

or

world

word
work
worm

72

ur

curly

curtain
hurry
curve

Say the word write. When w works with r , give no sound to w . See page 92.

sit

ki**ss**

bo**ss**y

Say these words.

saw	messy
say	dress
see	sailboat

YES, SIR...I WAS TOLD BY MY TEACHER TO COME TO YOUR OFFICE...

NO, I'VE NEVER BEEN HERE BEFORE.. I'VE NEVER DONE ANYTHING REALLY WRONG BEFORE......

YOU HAVE A NICE OFFICE..

HOW ARE YOU AND THE P.T.A. GETTING ALONG?

sk

skate

skip
skin
skid
ski

st

star

stand
story
stop

sm

smack

smell
small
smile

sw

swing

sweep
sweater
sweet

sl

sleep

slide
sleeve
slow

sp

spoon

sports
spot
spend

sn

Snoopy

sneeze
snail
snow

sc

scare

scout
scale
scooter

77

str

string

straw
street
strike

sh

shoe

fish
shell
shake
wash

Give no sound to the t in these words.

st

castle

whistle
listen

Sometimes you give **s** the same sound you give **z** when you say these words.

s

dai**s**y

ea**s**y
chee**s**e
plea**s**e

I LOVE PLAYING HOCKEY BALL!

79

teeth

ba**t**

wa**t**er

Say these words.

time   top

tail   tent

hat   kitten

I'VE GOTTA FIND THAT BLANKET, CHARLIE BROWN!

LUCY WON'T TELL ME WHERE SHE BURIED IT SO I'VE GOTTA DIG 'TIL I FIND IT!

I'VE JUST GOTTA DIG AN' DIG AN' DIG UNTIL I FIND IT!

GOOD LUCK!

81

tr   tree

trip
try
trunk

tw   twigs

twin
twice
twenty

We give different sounds to these **th** words when we say them.

th   bath

tooth
third
thin

th   mother

the
though
they

82

tion

atten**tion**

sta**tion**
vaca**tion**
ac**tion**

Sometimes we give **ed** at the end of a word the same sound we give **t** in bat.

ed

danc**ed**

laugh**ed**
promis**ed**
sock**ed**

OKAY, I'M READY... THROW ME THE HOCKEY BALL!

YOU INVITED HER.. I DIDN'T

pumpkin

music

Try saying this word giving the u the same sound you give the u in pumpkin.

Ughh!

Say it again giving the u the same sound you give the u in music.

Ugh!

Which way do you like to say it?

Say these words. Give the u
the same sound you give the
u in pumpkin.

cup   cut

drum   supper

umbrella   uncle

Here are more words. Give
the u the same sound you
give the u in music.

mule   cucumber

tune   cute

use   unicorn

There are other spellings for the sound you give the
u in music.

ue

avenue

cue

See page 93 for the ew spelling when you give it
the sound of u as in music.

Vv *Vv*

 **V**iolet

 sha**v**e

 ri**v**er

88

Say these words.

vine   view

visit   vase

velvet   valentine

WHAT A CRABBY BUG!

wagon

wash

world

When w works as a consonant it is often used before a vowel. Say these words and listen for the sound you give the w .

went	wag
wing	work
won	water

BOY, WHAT A DAY...THIS HAS BEEN THE WORST DAY OF MY LIFE!

I WOKE UP THIS MORNING LOOKING FORWARD TO THE SPELLING BEE, AND I END UP IN THE PRINCIPAL'S OFFICE.... GOOD GRIEF!

ON A DAY LIKE THIS, A PERSON REALLY NEEDS HIS FAITHFUL DOG TO COME RUNNING OUT TO GREET HIM ...

HERE'S THE WORLD WAR I PILOT IN HIS FIGHTER PLANE LOOKING FOR THE RED BARON!

SIGH

Give the w no sound when you say these words.

wr

write

wrestle
wrinkle
wrong
wrap

wh

wheels

whistle
why
when
where

Give the w no sound when you say these words.

wh

who

whom
whose
whole

Can you hear the different sounds you give wh in
the two sets of words?

Sometimes w **acts as a vowel.**

ow

throw

slow
know
show

ow

cow

how
now

ew

stew

few
new

aw

paw

law
saw

x-ray

mailbo**x**

Say these words.

fox   wax

mix   ax

fix   Mexico

RAKE
RAKE
RAKE

THAT'S **MY** BOOK YOU'RE READING!

IT IS SAID THAT ABRAHAM LINCOLN ONCE WALKED THROUGH A BLIZZARD TO RETURN A BORROWED BOOK

YOU WON'T EVEN WALK ACROSS THE ROOM!

I SHOULD HAVE LOANED MY BOOK TO ABRAHAM LINCOLN!

95

When x comes at the beginning of a word you often give it the sound you give to z .

x  xylophone

yawn

yacht

Say these words.

yes	**y**ell
yet	**y**ou
yellow	**y**esterday

NOBODY THINKS I CAN WIN THE CITY SPELLING BEE, SNOOPY, BUT I'M GONNA SHOW 'EM!

I NOT ONLY KNOW A LOT OF HARD WORDS, BUT I KNOW EVERY SPELLING RULE IN THE BOOK...

THE ONLY ONE I HAVE TROUBLE REMEMBERING IS, "I BEFORE E EXCEPT AFTER D"...OR IS IT, "E BEFORE I EXCEPT AFTER G"?

"I BEFORE B EXCEPT AFTER T"? "V BEFORE Z EXCEPT AFTER E"?

GOOD GRIEF!

99

Sometimes y is a vowel. In these words y is a vowel and you give it the sound you give i as in kite. See page 40.

y

sky

cry
my
dry
flying

In these words give the y the sound you give e in she. See page 26.

y

Peppermint Patty

party
Lucy
baby

Zz *Z z*

zz

zzzzz

Say these words.

zebra	zoo
lazy	zipper
fuzz	dozen

Sometimes we give words with s the same sound
we give to z . See page 79.

TO THE TEACHER:

Snoopy's Secret Code Book is designed to supplement any program of reading instruction and help students develop independence in word recognition and spelling. It is a valuable teaching aid to use with beginning students and a helpful resource book for others.

The names of the written vowel letters (graphemes) sometimes have little resemblance to the sounds (phonemes) which we bring to them. Here no effort is made to present all of the graphemic variations, but only those chiefly met in the written language of the early grades. While the sounds we give to consonants are more consistently represented by their spellings, here, also, we have only chosen those variant spellings which occur again and again in the written language of the students. **Snoopy's Secret Code Book,** then, deals with the more consistent spellings of the phonemes.

Snoopy's Secret Code Book introduces the students to the regularities of our spelling system and the most commonly used variant sounds and spellings.

Linguists generally agree that our writing system encodes the phonemes of speech. With **Snoopy's Secret Code Book** you can help students move from the oral language they know to recognition of the written symbols that represent this language—from speech to reading. Students learn that the sound is represented by the letter—or letters—rather than being taught that letters have sounds. A letter has no sound. Through a list of carefully selected words which are in the speaking vocabulary of most students, illustrated by cartoons, the students are able to decode many of the sounds we give to letters when we say them in words. The familiar cartoons are an aid to pronunciation, and free the student from asking someone to do it for him. A word and its meaning are gained at the same time—an important first step toward independent reading power.

In addition to the key words, other words are listed in Snoopy's doghouse to provide an opportunity for the student to apply the information gained through the picture clues. This method of presenting the words helps the pupil to reinforce his understanding that speech sounds, phonemes, can become written symbols, graphemes.

Say these words. Give the a in these words the same sound that you give the a in cap.

flag	and
crabby	grab
bat	candle

Say these words. Give the a in these words the same sound that you give to the a in cake.

hate	plane
face	date
cave	bake

If **Snoopy's Secret Code Book** is to be used as a resource book, you will want to introduce it to the entire class. When the students have had a few "trial-runs" to find words, you will easily identify students who need help before they can use the book independently. Those students who need to be strengthened in left to right progression and the use of configuration clues should be urged to SAY and WRITE the words.

If these following points are emphasized for the students, they can use **Snoopy's Secret Code Book** to help them pronounce and spell words.

1. The consonants and vowels are identified by color clues at the top of the page.

    Vowels have a **gold** band. The vowels are a, e, i, o, u, and sometimes y and w.

    Consonants have a **green** band. The consonants are b, c, d, f, g, h, j, k, l, m, n, p, q, r, s, t, v, w, x, y, and z.

2. Cartoons and words have matching clues shown in **red**.

gui**t**a**r**

3. Letters are listed in alphabetical order with the page numbers for reference.

    See page 5.

The bibliography includes books about phonics instruction, phonetic studies, and linguistics. Paperback books are marked with an asterisk.

Phonics instruction is not an end in itself, but, when used as a component of the total reading program it makes a valuable contribution. **Snoopy's Secret Code Book** gives help with phonics instruction in a way that will be interesting to students.

BIBLIOGRAPHY OF PHONICS MATERIALS

Austin, Mary C. and Morriton, Coleman, *The First R, The Harvard Report on Reading in Elementary Schools.* The Macmillan Co., 1963.

*Bagford, Jack, *Phonics: Its Role in Teaching Reading.* Sernoll, Inc., Iowa City, Iowa, 1967.

Bloomfield, Leonard or Clarence L. Barnhart, *Let's Read—A Linguistic Approach.* Wayne State University Press, 1961.

*Botel, Morton, *How To Teach Reading, Revised Edition* (pp. 53–107). Follett Publishing Company, 1963.

Cordts, Anna D., *Phonics For The Reading Teacher.* Holt, Rinehart and Winston, Inc., 1965.

DeBoer & Dallman, *Teaching of Reading* (pp. 80–91). Holt, Rinehart and Winston, Inc., 1960.

*Durkin, Dolores, *Phonics and the Teaching of Reading, Third Edition.* Bureau of Publications, Teachers College, Columbia University, 1968.

*Emans, Robert, "History of Phonics (pp. 602–608). *Elementary English,* May, 1968.

*Farr, Roger, *Reading: what can be measured?* International Reading Association Research Fund, 1969.

Fries, Charles C., *Linguistics and Reading.* Holt, Rinehart and Winston, Inc., 1963.

Gans, Roma, *Fact and Fiction About Phonics.* The Bobbs-Merrill Company, Inc., 1964.

Gleason, Henry A. Jr., *Linguistics and English Grammar.* Holt, Rinehart and Winston, Inc., 1965.

*Heilman, Arthur W., *Phonics in Proper Perspective.* Charles E. Merrill Books, Inc., 1966.

*Ibeling, F. W., "Supplementary Phonics Instruction & Reading and Speaking Ability" (pp. 152–156). *Elementary School Journal,* 62, 1961.

McKee, Paul, *The Teaching of Reading in the Elementary School* (Chapters 8–11). Houghton Mifflin Company, 1948.

*Scott, Louise B. and Thompson, Jesse J., *Phonics in Listening, in Speaking, in Reading, in Writing.* McGraw-Hill Book Company, 1962.

Smith, E. Brooks, Goodman, Kenneth S., and Meredith, Robert, *Language and Reading in the Elementary School.* Holt, Rinehart and Winston, Inc., 1970.